the **70**s

First published in 2006 by
Prion
an imprint of the
Carlton Publishing Group
20 Mortimer Street
London W1T 3JW

2 4 6 8 10 9 7 5 3

A catalogue record for this book is available from the British Library

ISBN-13: 978-1-85375-600-9
ISBN-10: 1-85375-600-8

Printed and bound in China

the 70s

The Decade That Style Forgot

Tracey Turner

PRION

Contents

CHARTS TOPPERS

BY anny fedora

Introduction

The 1970s were responsible for many things: Showaddywaddy,
The Partridge Family, Spangles, Noddy Holder's sidies, and the
musical genre that dare not speak its name: prog rock. Some,
like Space Dust, Space Hoppers and punk, are remembered fondly.
Others – Shakin' Stevens and pet rocks among them – are
remembered with a collective wince. But the true buttock-clenching
horror of the 70s lies in the many and varied crimes against style that
were perpetrated during the decade.

Why did the people of the 70s make so many ghastly style mistakes?
We may never know the real reason, but it's fair to say that they took
a *lot* of drugs during the 1960s. Whatever the cause, an almost univer-
sal lack of restraint, coupled with an absence of taste, led to some of
the most regrettable fashion *faux pas* of any era. Platform shoes? Let's
make them so that foolhardy wearers are teetering on the brink of an
abyss. Flared trousers? We'll need several metres of crimplene, some
iron-on transfers and a few rivets for each billowing bell-bottom.

Most people have, of course, set fire to any photographic evidence of
their grimmest fashion errors from the 70s. We have had to search far
and wide to track down the crotch-mangling, buttock-hugging,
avocado-and-dung-coloured polyester examples you see here. This book
is the result of a long and difficult search, and many of the photo-
graphs are previously unpublished, for obvious reasons. If you think you
can bear to revisit tank tops, fondue sets, white afros and bilious-green
bidets, simply turn the page.

Welcome to the fashion wasteland that was the 1970s.

Wakey Wakey!

In the 70s toilets were considered
naked without appropriate
shag-pile clothing. Preferably in puce.

Nightwear can be interpreted in all sorts of ways. It doesn't usually include a shirt, tie and trousers, but – hey – it's 1973, why not live a little?

It's hard looking natural modelling a woeful pair of Ys and a vest, but the heraldic backdrop is a big help. Especially for the guy holding the bugle.

Everything you could want in underwear – lurid tartan and paisley prints, and they're polyester. Wear them in the usual under-your-clothes sort of way or save money by doubling them up as swimwear.

Work

This guy's looking good and he knows it. He's certainly managed to grab the attention of these lovely polyester-clad ladies, even though he appears to have someone else's sideburns.

He's a hard-nosed businessman and he's wearing a tie that says, 'Yeah, it's bright apricot. Wanna make something of it?' His colleagues have made the mistake of forgetting their shades and are forced to cower in the background.

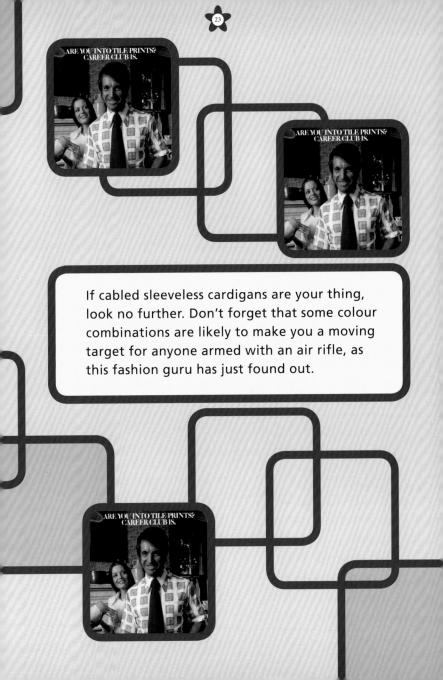

ARE YOU INTO TILE PRINTS?
CAREER CLUB IS.

ARE YOU INTO TILE PRINTS?
CAREER CLUB IS.

If cabled sleeveless cardigans are your thing, look no further. Don't forget that some colour combinations are likely to make you a moving target for anyone armed with an air rifle, as this fashion guru has just found out.

ARE YOU INTO TILE PRINTS?
CAREER CLUB IS.

This is a man who has scrutinised his choice of tie and found it more than satisfactory. He's not quite so sure of himself in the ladies' longer-length jumper, though.

Home

Very Susan Hampshire, very Sanderson.

You'd need at least three bottles of wine to take your mind of those trousers and that much pine.

I used to spend my dinner parties in the kitchen.

Hostess Imperial
£59.95 (incl VAT).
correct at time of going to press

'Now I can display and serve my sprouts at the dinner table, dispensing with the need for all that troublesome plate carrying. Plus we all get the chance to watch our desserts congealing and our coffee going cold while we tuck in to our main course.'

This migraine-inducing combination of floor and wall tiles is just one of the many attractions of this kitchen. Beige, isn't it? And there's even a handy niche for your fondue set.

Remember, avocado isn't just for the bathroom. These ladies are certainly impressed ... or could they have caught sight of themselves in a mirror?

When this couple aren't relaxing in their stylish lounge with their slide collection, they're congratulating themselves on having done their own conveyancing.
Loudly, at parties.

Keep moving, nothing to see here.

Sitting in this chair is like being engulfed by a dungheap. And it's cleverly designed as a hideous gurning face to frighten children. You wouldn't want to watch *Magpie* sitting on that, would you?

Kids

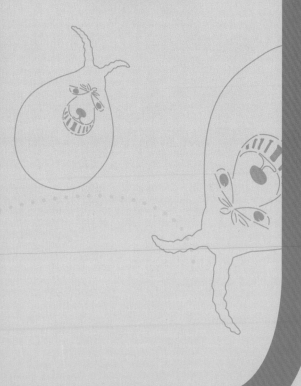

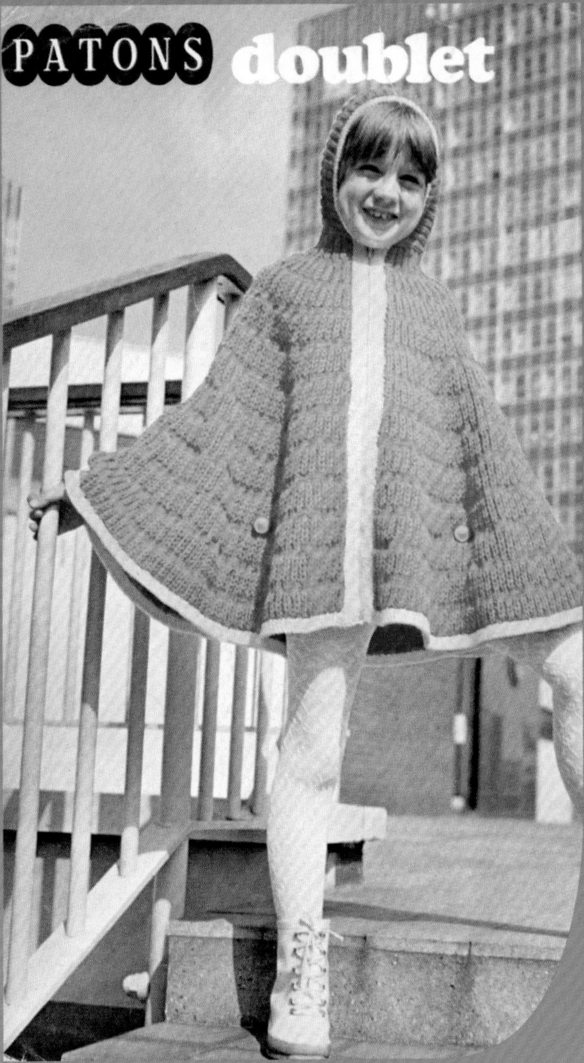
PATONS doublet

These expectant ladies all have a far-away look in their eyes. But being up the duff is no picnic, particularly when you're wearing puff-sleeved polyester.

The expression on this child's face gives new meaning to the phrase 'fashion victim'. Sadly, his mother is busy shopping for more garishly coloured clothing and wondering if there's anything more she can do to draw attention to her own buttocks.

You simply had to have a Chopper bike if you were a kid in the 70s. Too bad, then, that this kid's parents were too tight to get him one and opted for an imitation that earned him the ridicule of his peers. His little brother might be laughing now...

This little girl is grimly gritting her teeth to hide her smock-related pain. Touchingly, the other child summons up a smile despite the conclusion of her mother's threat to 'knit you one just like mine'.

On Holiday

This holiday-making family looks a bit on the glum side … until they discover a dead lobster: the perfect kiddies' toy, *and* it complements Mum's hotpants perfectly.

French men are renowned for their virility, but not wearing strides *that* snug. At least the tightly crotched couple haven't made a cravat error so common in visitors to the Continent.

… On the other hand, this man's cravat, stay-press white slacks and rock-hard demeanour have clearly made him irresistible to women. After hours of cat-fighting, these three have agreed to share.

These outsize specs may look ordinary but they have the power to convince the wearer that it's absolutely fine to dress in a hideous checked mini-dress exactly the same as your friends'. Still, one of the guys in the crotch-clinging strides likes their look. Unfortunately, he and his friends are incarcerated in their own trousers and unable to move.

If you're hoping to get into the girls' changing rooms, no amount of hairstyling and jewellery detracts from a beard, a hairy chest and an obvious penis. You're fooling no one.

Stay-cool nylon is the obvious choice for beach wear. Shrug on this wet-look maxi dress, add Rover's lead as an understated necklace, and go get orange!

'Eye-wateringly lurid' is the keynote to this season's summer fashions. But there's no need to go to these lengths to show off your Immac skills. Doesn't that pinch?

63

Jantzen

A source of pride

JANTZEN, INC. PORTLAND, OREGON 97208 AND VANCOUVER, B.C. V5T3J3

Why not turn those tired old polyester curtains into stunning holiday outfits? Here, the theme is 'hospital worker'.

Can you think of anything more terrifying than a sing-along with these people?

The satin-effect paisley dressing-gown brings a certain *je ne sais quoi* to the frilly-shirt-and-bow tie combination. Phew, this guy's a ladykiller. Meanwhile, the denim safari jacket and bell-bottoms seem to have already had a devastating effect. Steady on, love.

These three hotties are a girl's dream however they're dressed, but wearing nothing but their undies and a pair of shades they're nigh-on irresistible.

Outdoor Pursuits

PATONS

Tank Tops
33 - 40 in. (84 - 101 cm)

to knit

and crochet

The tank top: need we say more?

These people are attempting to look like a wholesome family group in their chunky knits, but the fact that Dad is obviously a member of the Village People ruins the effect.

The white afro: arguably hairdressing's most regrettable moment.

If your aim is to make people sink to the ground sobbing uncontrollably, this scarlet wet-look nylon jacket, with its matching rakish cap, is for you. Stalk menacingly out of the undergrowth for maximum effect.

Run for your lives! There's an upper-class, bewildered-looking maniac on the loose armed with a hunting rifle. Don't you realise those smoking jackets are like a red rag to a bull?

If you're middle aged and horribly out of condition, chunky knits and leather jackets are not going to fool anyone into thinking you're a member of *The Professionals*.

Every wardrobe should include a triffid-patterned afghan in bilious green 'suedette' and fake fur. The only dilemma is whether or not to opt for sleeves.

Large-check pantaloons, the top half of a gorilla suit, ginger-and-white *faux* fur ... no wonder these guys look pleased with themselves.

Getting Ready

Avocado-coloured baths, cork floor tiles, a bathing blonde wearing lots of blue eyeshadow ... all of it says '70s bathroom chic'. After a heavy night those matching soft furnishings are designed to hit you between the eyes like a charging rhino.

This woman may look happy in her bath, with her many toiletries, the handy bath-side niche and the telephone within easy reach, but an electrical appliance that close to the water is an accident waiting to happen. At least her brain isn't battery-powered like the unfortunate woman opposite. Nice hat, though.

The secret to a resplendent outfit is in the detail. That means footwear and undercrackers. This chap's wearing his lucky pants, and combined with a pair of comfy clogs and his Christmas socks, the world's his oyster.

Being forced to wear the shire-horse shirt was the last straw for Malcolm. Just after this photograph was taken he set fire to the curtains, destroyed the furniture with his *Crackerjack* consolation prize and was never seen again.

Going
Out

Ladies, please! You're simply playing into the hands of permed delinquents like this one. He loves it when you parade around in your hotpants and unbutton your matching shirts for no good reason. Think of him and cover yourselves up, for the love of God.

The woodland spirits have been speaking to the woman on the left. They've been telling her to *leave them alone*. And do something about that unsightly crotch creasing while she's at it.

There's evil intent in this man's eye. He buys his victims a drink, then uses the strange effect of the light on his tie to hypnotise them.

These women are unprepared for his advances, but luckily they've come dressed in a fabric that'll give that tie a run for its money. If they bump into the woman on page 103 the effect will be devastating.

These lovelies adopt a different but no more subtle defence in this hellish shade of orange.

She's escaped Mr Hypno-tie from page 100 but she's fallen prey to an obvious silent-film villain. In the time it takes to twirl his moustache he'll have her tied to the nearest railway tracks.

We all make mistakes, but deliberately giving the world a grandstand view of your ta-tas is asking for trouble. And it looks like they've found it: the bow-tie twins have just changed the plans for their double date.

What a touching tribute. But perhaps the rivets were an unwise choice of material?

Boot-time story!!

Time and place – here and now. All-star cast of supple leathers, super wet-looks, silky suedes. Happy ending? Of course there is – see the next eleven pages!

Wet-look, pull-on boot in man-made material with a cling stretch leg and smooth foot. Foam lined for comfort, with an elasticated top. Decorative tie trim. Durable sole, heel 2ins high, leg height 13ins. **Red, brown, white or black.** **LH 881 Boots**

Sizes and half-sizes 4 to 6 £8·50 20 wks 43p

State size and colour required

Some people will do anything to get noticed, but the orange bowler hats and hotpants is a step too far for most people. On the other hand, in this remarkable jewelled creation at least you're never going to feel under-dressed.

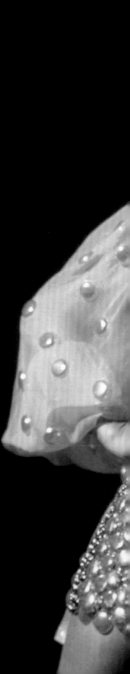

Seeking that mysterious, devil-may-care look coupled with a ladies' hairdo? Add an element of danger with a razor-blade motif.

Platforms just aren't platforms unless health and safety regulations stipulate wearing a hard hat if you leave the house in them.

Bedtime

Z Z Z Z Z

If you want to make bedtime a sea of billowing nylon, try this range of shock-inducing nighties. Note the importance of elaborate coiffure for this look.

Z

Wake U

Men's pjs never looked more alluring than this pastel polyester-mix selection. Let's hope they're not getting into bed together, or with the nylon nightie women: they could spontaneously combust.

Planning a seduction? This lady certainly knows how to soften the mood, with her flowing robe, shag-pile carpeting and come-hither eyes.

Pretty Irresistible

at only £11·95 (plus postage, packing 65p)

Brighten your days and evenings by zipping into this beautifully styled house-coat.

This fashionable garment is available in three gorgeous colour combinations and made from 100% cotton fabric in a towelling velour finish that's fabulously soft to the touch, and luxurious to look at.

Cosily warm in winter, refreshingly cool in summer and so absorbent that it is perfect after swim-wear too.

Cut to flatter all figures the house-coat is fully machine washable. Its incredibly low price should tempt you to buy more than one.

Home Paraphern

Please send me the items indicated.
House Coat(s) @ £12.60 inc. ☐ F167–Jade   ☐ F168–Ma
State second choice of colour
☐ X15–Catalogue(s) @ 30p with or without order.
Telephone orders accepted 24 hrs a day, 7 days a week. Credit

There's no point in planning a seduction dressed in one of these hideous towelling caftans. You have to admire the little fringes at the bottom, though.

Easy Care
washable
drip dry
non-iron

LILAC AND WHITE

ALL WHITE

ROSE AND WHITE

TERYLENE

Easy Care
washable
drip-dry
non-iron

Vantona

You're probably thinking of ways to make your own bedroom a vision of frilly man-made fabrics. As a direct result of this sort of thing the fire brigade was permanently on red alert during the 70s.

Picture Credits

The publishers would like to thank the following sources for their kind permission to reproduce the pictures in this book:

Corbis: /Bettmann: 69, /Lynn Goldsmith: 76, /Stock4B: 50,51

FotoLibra: /Pawle Calvert-Brown: 44, /Bernard Howden: 49, /Richard Morris: 92-93, /Sabine Oppenlander: 58, 95, 98, /William Pears: 128

Getty Images: /Taxi/Richard Bradbury: 112

Photos 12: /interfoto: 52

Private Collection: 45

Rex Features: 62, 115, 108-9, /Andre Csillag: 97, /Keystone USA: 113, /Gunnar Larsson: 53, 73, 96, 104, /Jon Lyons: 83, /Sipa: 90

The Advertising Archive Ltd: 4, 6, 9, 10, 11, 12, 13, 14, 15, 19, 22, 23, 24-25, 27, 28, 29, 30-31, 32, 33, 34-35, 36, 37, 39, 40-41, 46, 47, 56, 57, 60-61, 63, 64, 65, 66-67, 68, 70-71, 74, 75, 77, 78, 79, 80-81, 82, 85, 86, 87, 88, 89, 91, 99, 100, 101, 102, 103, 105, 108, 122, 123, 116-7, 118-9, 120-1, 124-5, 126-7

Topfoto.co.uk: 17, 20-21, 42-43, 54-55, 106-7, 110-1,

Every effort has been made to acknowledge correctly and contact the source and/or copyright holder of each picture and Carlton Books Limited apologises for any unintentional errors or omissions that will be corrected in future editions of this book.